In Wait for the Perfect Sky

(1998-2019)

COLLECTED POETRY

BY GAURAV BHATIA

In Wait for the Perfect Sky

WIZARD OF WORDS PUBLISHING L.L.C.
745 Barclay Cir
Unit 310
Rochester MI 48307

ISBN-13: 978-0-578-57848-4

I dedicate this book to the five women in my life
without whom this book would not have been possible.

My teacher, Mrs. Renu Gulati, whose early
encouragements helped spark in me a lifelong
love for the English language.

My Mother, Mrs. Anita Bhatia, who never got tired of
collecting the scraps of paper on which
I tend to write when inspiration strikes.

My Wife, Rohini Kamakoti, without whose
amazing support I would not have found
the time to write in the first place.

And finally, my two beautiful daughters,
Sanjana – *The Girl With the Flower*
and Anjali – *Girl Wild.*

My sincere thanks to all my family, friends
and other hapless audience whose critique
over the years helped polish the rhymes.
To them I say:

If my sharp wit has ever offended
so too my verse have often mended

Contents

The Optimist

Amidst chaos rife

the optimist lives his life

marching to his fife

holding hopes up high

a better tomorrow is nigh

where real dreams abound

and life choices redound

the days go by-and-by

in wait for the perfect sky

The Girl with the Flower

A little girl stood in my garden
and plucked a flower without my pardon
as I watched her from the shade
quietly observing the flower's beauty fade

Then I bid her to come hither
as she too watched the flower wither
and asked her if it won't have been better
to leave the flower in its mortal tether?

The little girl pondered on this problem
as she sadly watched the wilting blossom
an assumption she was wrong in making
that the flower's beauty was for taking

The girl wished that she had the power
to turn back time and revive the flower
so giving her some seeds, and my pardon
I watched hope replanted in my garden

Girl Wild

Girl Child, Girl Wild

princess, self styled

whose reindeer games once riled

yet innocence too beguiled

ray of golden sunshine

in a world otherwise defiled

Blessed were those days we whiled

when rainbows bloomed and flowers smiled

girl child, girl reviled

princess, self styled

stay blessed, stay wild

always by my side

A Walk in the Woods

Once upon an early morning
as the new day was aborning
my dog and I headed outdoor
I was bent on strenuous walking
the dog intent on strenuous stalking
in woods we'd never seen before
a new place, and nothing more

The air stung of calefaction
the path was beaten to compaction
from feet that passed here before
the going got ever steeper
as the woods got ever deeper
and my feet, tired and sore
from strenuous walking, and nothing more

The dog ran ahead, his bondage severed
while to keep pace, I endeavored
failing miserably in the chore
when quickly my fortunes mended
for suddenly the woods were ended
and we stumbled on a moor
an open space, and nothing more

Flowers bloomed amongst the bracken
and my pace couldn't help but slacken
and take in this vision of yore
amazing that in chaos urban
ever encroaching life suburban
such beauty could yet endure
nature's grace, and nothing more

Birds of every color envisioned
in bush and tree positioned
sang their feathered score
while the dog and I examined
creatures furtive and determined
scurrying across the forest floor
nature raw, and nothing more

From our reverie, we were startled
as bushes nearby parted
and out stepped a creature of lore
a royal stag with horns of velvet
equally startled, made his exit
and disappeared without scent or spoor
nature's way, and nothing more

Eventually, we came upon a valley
that we added to our tally
of wondrous things we had seen before
mist flowed from every corner
draped over flowing water
with ferns growing across the shore
nature's fence, and nothing more

Alas the sun was quickly waning
and there were still miles remaining
between here and to my door
so we took our leave belated
though I know we left unsated
our eyes shall hunger, evermore
our eyes shall hunger, evermore
for nature's beauty, and nothing more

About Dogs

Willing to follow where you roam

always the first to welcome you home

giving comfort whenever you need

knows your mood though you may not heed

Never the one to hold a grudge

choosing to forgive than to judge

gentle beast with one desire

to earn your love but never your ire

Watching your back in company of strangers

a creature of fury if you are in danger

this bond is an ancient and selfish trend

between man and his self-less friend

The Migrant

Hush child, avert your gaze

they have set your home ablaze

your kin destroyed like mice

never forget their sacrifice

to give you this chance to thrive

the jackboots, do you hear them coming?

Run Child! Keep on Running!

Brave the heat, fight the thirst

my child, survive you must

remember those you left behind

as you journey through lands unkind

refuge you shall only find

in the shining city atop the hill

so make your way towards the light

Run Child! Run all Night!

15

Head for the city that offers succor

to the tired, needy and poor

an example for the world to be

from sea to shining sea

where at last you can be free

the city is now within your reach

harden your resolve and steel your will

Run Child! Run up the hill!

What's this? A closed door?

where there was only mercy before

the man at the gate points to a new decree

that only the wealthy can be free

the rest shall be turned back at the quay

stay quite and wait for the dark

the light is out yet there remains a spark

but if ever you hear the jackboots coming

Run Child! And Never Stop Running!

About Envy

I often wonder of the reason, for envy having
no fixed season, 'tis present the year round

its influence is widely ranging, never waning,
never changing, such persistence does astound

Well known is the figment, of envy having
certain pigment, viridescent belike

Yet envy is far from visible, ever drawn
to divisible, ensnaring friend and foe alike

It'd be a glaring omission if envy was mistaken for
ambition, for the two could not have more differed

Of success, envy is contemptuous, yet of its fruits
'tis covetous, dismissing the sacrifices incurred

Dear Friend, do heed my warning, beware of those
given to fawning, while barely holding their bile

For indeed there is something slithering,
something churning, something withering,
hidden beneath that smile

Being Human

Life in totality
is a journey all too brief
with an ever looming finality
so why the drama and grief
over my frail and fluid morality?

I have refused to follow
these rules of your making
knowing your promises to be hollow
their legitimacy was difficult to swallow
I knew the rules were for breaking

You have nothing with which to bind me
neither norm nor convention
shame does not blind me
for pride never confined me
with false hopes of ascension

I do not care if I exist
by divine will or happenstance
it is not society I resist
but loss of freedom and chance

to be human, just for once

The Jaded

Soul, oh soul come back to me!
for you should have never left my shell
and allowed me to fill it instead
with shiny, sordid gifts of hell

I sought to shake the devil's hand
in name of the greater good
to the detriment of my fellow man
I abandoned that for what I stood

Lately when I look in the mirror
it's a stranger who looks back at me
a cruel face with jaded eyes
devoid of all humanity

Soul, oh soul come back to me!
and bring with you the innocence of youth
the ignorance of lofty ideals
now marred forever by squalid truth

Three Angels

Ever since birth, I have
lived with angels three
to know the good and bad
pleasure you've already had
the third is known as Free

The good angel strives to keep
me virtuous to my marrow
so that night or day
may I never once stray
from the path of straight and narrow

The bad angel on the other hand
does the opposite as expected
he tempts me with fruit forbidden
and promise of life with pleasures smitten
where all guilt may be rejected

It's said a man's worth is known
by the angel's voice he hears,
ever virtuous or forever smudged
by his peers, the man is judged
on the path to which he adheres

Yet I hear that forgotten voice
of angel number three
that says it matters not, win or lose
which angel's voice I choose
just as long as that choice is Free

About Ambition

In the winter of life

my mind ponders

on this morbid thought

All that I am

and all I have been

shall be for naught

Fame, power

and fortune

I have always sought

27

Undisputed master

of all that

could be bought

Though many feats

and mighty deeds

I may have wrought

Greater are

the miracles

that the world forgot

If a lesson through

crumbling castles

could be taught

Nature of things is

to fail and fall

in dust and rot

So what has a lifetime

of ambition

truly begot?

To my great shame

An answer

I have not

The Poet

Of late I have been subject to some ridicule

for the volume of my rhymes has been minuscule

and if that's not enough to make one contrite

I have been asked why I even bother to write

As a poet, I am not prolific

for my work tends to be specific

I only write when something stirs my passion

birthing verse needlessly is not my fashion

As to the question why

you might as well question the blue sky

or changing of seasons

nature of things require no reasons

31

I write simply to satisfy my soul

beauty of the verse makes me whole

and if my sharp wit has ever offended

so too my verse have often mended

The Dragon

A prince rode forth
from his castle
on a noble quest
equipped with sword
a trusty horse
and his Sunday best

Rumor he had heard
of princess fair
a damsel in distress
held captive
by a winged fiend
in a lonely fortress

The road was long
the path unkind
yet on he pressed
the brave prince
intent to pass
this hardy test

After many feats
over glen and dale
at last he stood
across the castle
filled with dread
and fortitude

His challenge was
quite steeped
in pomp and flair
yet it did the trick
and drew the creature
from its lair

The dragon hovered
above our hero
and politely inquired
if he were lost
and what directions
the prince required?

"Release the princess!
or prepare to die!"
the prince demanded
what awe!
what virility
the prince commanded!

The dragon pled
its ignorance
of her whereabouts
and invited the prince
to search the castle
and settle his doubts

Though he searched
high and low
through the dragon's lair
of the princess
the prince could find
neither hide not hair

Ah! but the clever prince
he did guess
the creature's trap
the civil tone was
just presage
for its jaws to snap

Undoubtedly it was
in the beast's maw
the tragic end
of the maiden fair
whose likely death
should be avenged

Of the wily worm
such treachery
is to be expected
it goes to show
that the race of worms
just can't be trusted

Wishing to make
in the morn
an early start
without further ado
he stabbed the dragon
through the heart

As it fell dying
the dragon spoke
its final words
"You have erred sir!
for the truth stands
in obverse"

VEGANISM

About Voters

Do voters care

if government sins

in their name?

Do voters' heads

then hang together

in collective shame?

Do voters ever

truly accept

their share of blame?

Or to a voter, politics

is akin to foetor

it's all the same?

VOTER
VOTER
VOTER
VOTER

About Patriotism

Question not what

we the leaders can do

for you

In fact we strongly prefer

no questions

about our actions

The state is law

the state is might

always right

Wave your flag, citizen

and abandon reason

for patriotism blind

as deadly as treason

The Politician

If a man promises you a world

where truth reigns and justice prevails

It's likely a politician you have encountered

a purveyor of tall tales

Beware! for here is the proverbial wolf

clothed as you and me

seeking total dominion

in multiples of three

He will charm you with his fables

and many an anecdote

and pretend that you matter

as he begs for your vote

43

He will play the tune of prejudice

he will play to your deepest fears

and soon have you frothing

as he peddles his noxious wares

You shall be awed by his prowess

the seemingly endless ardor

and declare him to be your savior

the knight in shining armor

Alas once you pledge your vote

which is your right as a denizen

you will likely see his august back

disappearing over the horizon

Perhaps then the fog will lift
and sad truth shall dawn
in the political game of chess
we the sheeple are but pawns

But what if this man is not a wolf
but honest to goodness sheep
responding to a higher calling
with promises he means to keep?

What a remarkable creature
a rare and noble breed
Sadly its political tenure
would be short lived indeed

For on this particular subject
dear Darwin was quite succinct
in nature rarity is an aberration
and thus bound to go extinct.

The Rich

I don't believe in being charitable
I say this with the utmost sincerity
good karma is just a fable
fate does not seek parity

It's not a crime to amass wealth
only to spend it on pursuits shallow
pleasures denied to self
is the folly of youth callow

Kindness is a sentiment overrated
'Tis to be banished from the heart
The tired, the poor and the ill fated
I say each to his own compart

Wealth is more than just an object
for when all else I must waive
it shall be the means for me to resurrect
and keep apologizing from beyond the grave

My Father the Poet

Alas my father is a poet!
I wish he was a painter instead
for paintings tend to draw admirers
while verses usually fill them with dread

It's both comical and heart wrenching
when in a gathering father whips out his prose
and guests dive out through windows
if there happens to be a stampede at the doors

I can't say I blame them
for I too am victim of rhyme
suffering father's prolific verse
accompanied by pantomime

I know it hurts his pride
"boors! philistines!" he rumbles
unable to take rejection in his stride
for weeks at end he grumbles

If only my father made paintings
instead of birthing verses deep
there is little need for a wordsmith
in a world where words are cheap

Poems

Karma Bites

God created man
presumably in his image
an effort vain that pays
to its maker, no homage
of God, man has no further use
divinity is relegated to the obtuse
for science has heavens in its sights
Karma bites

Man created intelligence
presumably in his image
albeit artificial
a notion farcical
the circle shall thus be complete
when intelligence deems men obsolete
and humanity falls from blinding heights
Karma bites

About Women

A woman's love is beautiful

to which none dare compare

her passion, her desire

as fierce as fire

an angel's soul laid bare

A woman's hate is terrible

to which none dare compare

her fury, her ire

more fierce than fire

of which angels too despair

Nightmares

Nightmares! Nightmares!

the lonely, pitiful screams

float ever closer across bloody streams

those strange paths of twisted dreams

The mind draws a horrid track

across dreamscapes of torrid black

a shadow rises from the crimson sheen

stoking primal fears of the unseen

When the nights are dark and deep

in the sleeping mind they creep

and proceed to serve the vilest fare

glimpses of Satan's lair

Nightmares! Nightmares!

Valentine

I bought her flowers
for valentine
to offer up
this heart of mine

As I walked up slowly
to the gate
I dared to hope
I wasn't too late

For though we've had
many dances
So far I'd missed
every one of my chances

So now perhaps
the grace of the rose
would make up for
my lack of prose

I waited in her office
watching the clock tick
when right on cue
she called in sick

About Lawyers

I made a devil's bargain

With a lawyer clad in black

For I'd lost something to treachery

And he promised to win it back

He claimed he was a champion

Of righting what was wrong

He said that his services

Cost little more than a song

He promised to go to battle

Armed with legal verbose

And bring this sad saga

To a rapid close

Alas his actual deeds

Turned out to be a far cry

For his talent really lay

In simply sucking me dry

He charged me by the minute

He charged me by the hour

His charged just for thinking of me

While he sang in his shower

Time wore on with little done

My patience wore thinner still

So he lectured me about perseverance

Which only added to my bill

Oh I made a devil's bargain

With a lawyer clad in black

Who knew it'd cost a pound

Just to win a penny back

In the Age of Specialization

In the age of specialization

I've had to see

Doctors for my trouble

All separately

One for my errant throat

Second for my nose

A third for my ears

Though why, God only knows

The low point came

To my annoyance poignant

When each nostril required

A separate appointment

God is Dead

The never ending bloodshed

petulance wide spread

it can only be said

that God is dead

His abandoned creation

is plagued with fixation

of other's natural persuasion

and self righteous condemnation

Evil' s stunning rise

the silence of the wise

can only lead one to surmise

of God's demise

Yet a millennia of strife

with hatred rife

begs the question

that cuts like a knife

was God ever alive?

The Flight

Up, Up and away

on metal wings aloft

soar, soar through the wind

and swirling clouds soft

Stay, Stay unaware

of the howling night

pray, pray in the air

for that stable flight

Sink, Sink in descent

a terrible spiral deep

blink, blink and it's time

to rest in eternal sleep

About India

India is...you see

A phenomenon that was never meant to be

Far too long, far too wide

has stretched the never ending divide

between cultural issues and political opinions

and the very identity of faceless billions

North, south, east or west

A never ending saga of unrest

A nation with history enraptured

And a future, forever fractured

A people susceptible to illusion

with a fervor that borders on delusion

a government that takes pride in its gumption

to legitimize all forms of corruption

A culture fixated on division

with passion rivaling any mathematician

religion, color, race or cast

lineage and ancestors past

language, dialect or accent

income and social placement

Indians can never be satisfied

until in a category one has been classified

such customary majuscule

is often precursor to Divide and Rule

70

India is well...a fallacy

a phenomenon that was never meant to be

and yet for all our faults

We are still here...as you can see

The Curse of Knowledge

In the forgotten days of history
Life used to hold mystery
when new lessons were learnt every day
and hard won was every victory

There were pools of knowledge to garner
and magic just around the corner
the feeling that nothing was impossible
and of destiny, we the sole owner

Today, that world has faded
or is it us who are jaded?
fallen we have in the rat race
that once seemed so degraded

Somewhere we lost that magic
and knowingly which is indeed tragic
bitten we are with the curse of knowledge
trapped in a world so pelagic

Bitter is the taste of victory
when all you are left with is history
and a future where nothing is impossible
and no such thing as mystery

Eyes

I see the early morning sky

I feel the gentle morning breeze

And watch the sun reflected in your eyes

Shining, Shimmering Green!

Dark pools of unearthly light

And dreams yet unseen

The noon sun is riding high

I watch a glorious day unfold

And watch the sun reflected in your eyes

Brightly blazing Gold!

Luminous spheres enmeshed with light

And secrets yet untold

75

The evening hour is nigh at hand

And still enchanted I do stand

And watch the sun reflected in your eyes

Crystal china blue!

With swirling clouds in purple haze

And colors changing hue

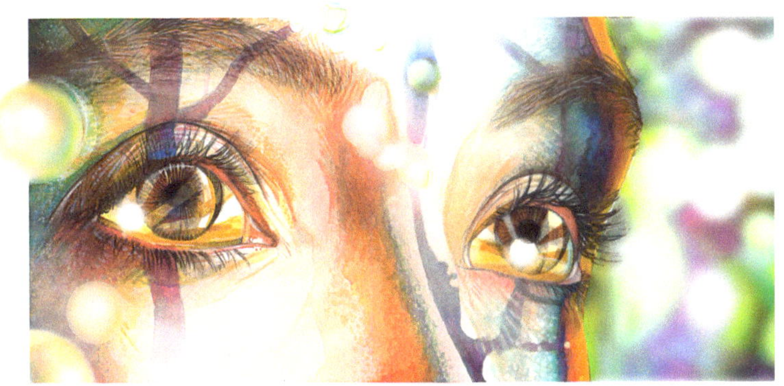

A Flight of Dreams

I befriended a little bird
and asked her how it felt to fly
soaring uninhibited at will
across the endless blue sky

Surely it must seem divine
to walk atop the swirling clouds
and ride the winds of fortune
unfettered from fear and doubt?

I wondered if the glittering stars
called out to my friend by name
whilst she flew past the moon
and beyond to worlds unnamed

The little bird waited patiently
for my fantasy to run its flow
knowing why I dreamt of places
where in waking I cannot go

Mirror Mirror

Mirror Mirror on the wall
in a dusty old hall
with silvery strings adorned
dreaming of days bygone

Once sought by mighty kings
your mortal playthings
who blinded by greed and hate
failed to know the evil at their gate

Now covered with dust and pollen
how the once mighty have fallen
shattered by time's relentless flacks
forever marred by unsightly cracks

Mirror Mirror on the wall
in a dusty old hall
gone are the heady days of power
evil shall often self devour

The Road Called Success

A bird in hand is worth two in bush
or so our thoughts are trained
inertia, veiled as security
is in our minds ingrained

Success is a path through a mighty desert
with never a chance of rain
a place where few dare to venture
and from which fewer emerge again

I too have long walked this path
with a half filled cup in my hand
some victories, twice as many defeats
are my marks upon the sand

What's kept me going all this while
is the proverbial cup of age
half empty for most, but in my eyes
that other half is faith

GOALS
AMBITIONS
DREAMS

The Recipe

Take a seed of thought
planted in your mind
turn it in to inspiration
and with effort combined

Add a dose of courage
and a spoonful of faith
then take destiny's ladle
and all of these conflate

Now set the dial on the oven
to the intensity you desire
the mixture of your hopes and dreams
must pass the test of fire

Timing is both your friend and enemy
for when you re-open that grate
too early will be just as disastrous
as opening it too late

About Perspective

A newborn's view of the world around

is limited to the feel and sound

of the mother's voice and gentle touch

universe contained in a little hutch

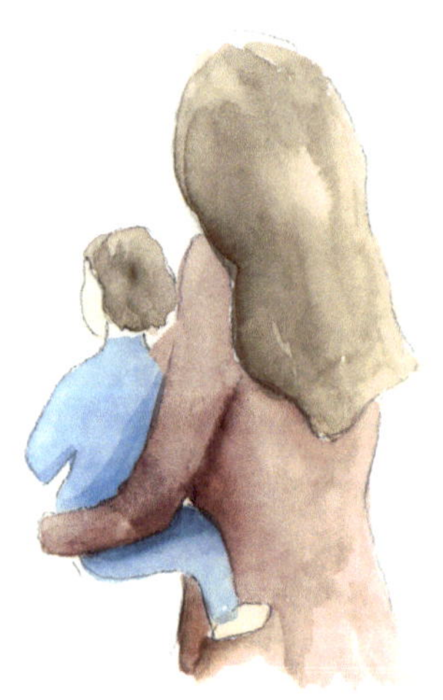

A toddler's view of the world

is somewhat more unfurled

recognizing no rules or censor

an explorer starting to venture

on a solo adventure

A teen's view of the world

tends to be constantly swirled

a plane of magical illusion

love and heartbreaks in profusion

a compendium of confusion

The world viewed from someone's mind

who has finally left the teens behind

seems to be an impossible juggle

of responsibilities in constant shuffle

a never ending struggle

The world view of the more matured

erstwhile jugglers, now chronically bored

after a lifetime of chasing perfection

tends to turn towards introspection

bittersweet memories in reflection

And finally the world viewed by the old

from breaking dawn to twilight gold

perhaps they understand it best

as they turn their sights away from this plane

and prepare to depart to the next

One world with so many hues

of ever changing point of views

differentiated by objective

the only constant in our lives

is the ever changing perspective

Lampshade

The party is in full swing
with merriment gaining ground from staid
but I stand aloof from the crowd
observing her from behind the lamp shade

This is not the first time I have seen her
we have crossed paths before
and every chance meeting has undeniably
left me wanting more

Sweet music fills the room
as she dances in rhythm to the euphony
her laughter rising above all other
as if aware of my heart's silent mutiny

Perhaps someday I will find the courage
to walk up and ask her for the next dance
instead of wondering what could have flourished
had I played the game of chance

But alas tonight is not that night
for my inner doubt just would not be swayed
perhaps we will dance another time
tonight I'll just watch from behind the lamp shade

The Man who Spoke in Haste

I lost the object of my love

By opening up my heart

But then she'd asked me to speak the truth

And I was honest from the start

Perhaps it was my eagerness

To share my world with her

In retrospect, I rushed too fast

as hindsight concurs

There was a man, who spoke in haste

Just to satisfy a whim

I hold more hope for a fool in love

Than I'll ever hold for him

The Temp

How the time has gone by

It's time to say goodbye

and move on to my next adventure

I've enjoyed our days

But now we must part ways

Such is my chosen indenture

What the future shall hold

Can never truly be told

But of one thing I'm certain

As sure as rain

Our paths will meet again

Somewhere beyond the curtain

Superstition

A rabbit's foot brings good luck
your fate the stars can tell
yet beneath a ladder you must never duck
lest fortune bids farewell

Take care to never spill salt
or you shall watch your destiny moulder
yet bad luck you may exalt
by throwing salt across your shoulder

A black cat in your path is cause for fear
but an itchy eye can go either way
the right promises that success is near
and the left foretells dismay

Deep are the roots of superstition
far deeper than the murky oceans
this chronic search for prediction
and hope in magic potions

Watershed

In the primordial soup
inanimate amidst the stoup
suddenly a tremor, a thrill
touch of divine will
something came alive
aware and intent to survive
keen to evolve and derive
as on to the shores it tread
Watershed

The air ruled by feather and craw
the earth ruled by tooth and claw
amidst these a helpless primate
itself destined to rule and predate
armed with reason and sight
from the trees did alight
learned to walk upright
as out of the cradle it led
Watershed

The reign of the sabertooth grew
each night brought terrors anew
when the heavens' tears and ire
led to the discovery of fire
there was now illumination
a tool to fight predation
of fear, a sweet cessation
as forever the darkness fled
Watershed

Tools from rock were hewn
clothes from skin were sewn
fur for coats was shorn
shells to arms adorn
thus the primate's zeal
led Fortuna to reveal
the secret of the wheel
as onwards humanity sped
Watershed

Through sword, stone, and academe
man now reigned supreme
an age to experiment and explore
civilizations galore
the spoken word was inscribed
complex thought transcribed
to the masses described
as wisdom thus spread
Watershed

Faith was long an excursion
the means to a spiritual incursion
a somewhat private affair
with minimal pomp and flair
and then religion was born
faith on the sleeve was worn
the fabric was forever torn
as god and government were wed
Watershed

Dark is the history page
for dark were the deeds of that age
when rational thoughts were banished
knowledge from this world vanished
replaced by fear and superstition
fables of suffering and perdition
self-serving rendition
as on sheep, the shepherds fed
Watershed

At last, the dogma was worn
a new age was finally born
an era of science and invention
a race to break convention
harnessing the power of steam
exploiting every seam
achieving every dream
as on the clouds, we tread
Watershed

Beneath success did jealousy breed
for conflict is man's true creed
the just rose in defiance
to a cruel and unholy alliance
soon the world was at war
destruction near and afar
brother against brother did spar
as all humanity bled
Watershed

From its ashes, a new world arose
the eagle now watched over the rose
man left his cocoon
and aimed to touch the moon
scientific wonders instilled
while the world was rebuilt
a prophecy fulfilled
as we played God instead
Watershed

The wars came home to roost
a tragedy self-induced
the scuffle between powers
crumbled the twin towers
innocence forever lost
freedoms forever tossed
a terrible cost
as bigotry raised its ugly head
Watershed

A world on brink of extinction
its rulers fixated on the distinction
between borders, color, and breed
victim of their own greed
the seas threaten to rise
fire, to rain from the skies
harbingers of man's demise
as our fate hangs by a thread
Watershed

A barren and desolate landscape
that the howling winds do scrape
of life, light, and sound devoid
the core of our world destroyed
pride came before the fall
a holocaust that destroyed all
scourge that consumed all
as to the stars, humanity fled
Watershed

On a world far away
a place still in nature's sway
suddenly a tremor, a thrill
touch of divine will
something came alive
aware and intent to survive
keen to evolve and derive
as in the womb, it bred
Watershed

The Mighty Niagara

Nature's fury vent

Rage that won't be spent

To nature's will, ye bent

Lest like the rock thee rent

About the Author

Gaurav Bhatia is a Canadian author, information technology whiz, serial entrepreneur and self-styled comedian. His work across multiple themes broadly addresses narratives of the human experience.

Gaurav has a panache for travel, aviation and all good things life has to offer. He loves to share his unique perspective on life through poetry.

Gaurav lives with his wife, two daughters and two dogs in Rochester, Michigan.

www.ingramcontent.com/pod-product-compliance
Lightning Source LLC
Chambersburg PA
CBHW040252301225
37435CB00040B/155